I0467376

DELICIOUSLY SCRUMPTIOUS CUP-CAKES

Food Coloring Book

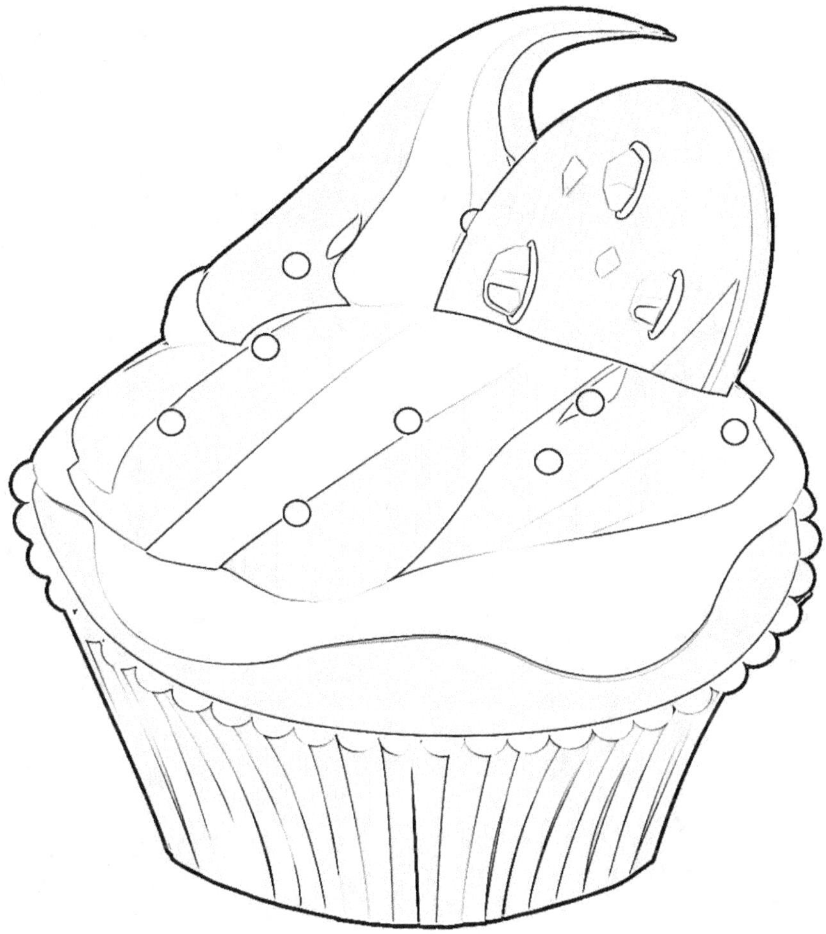

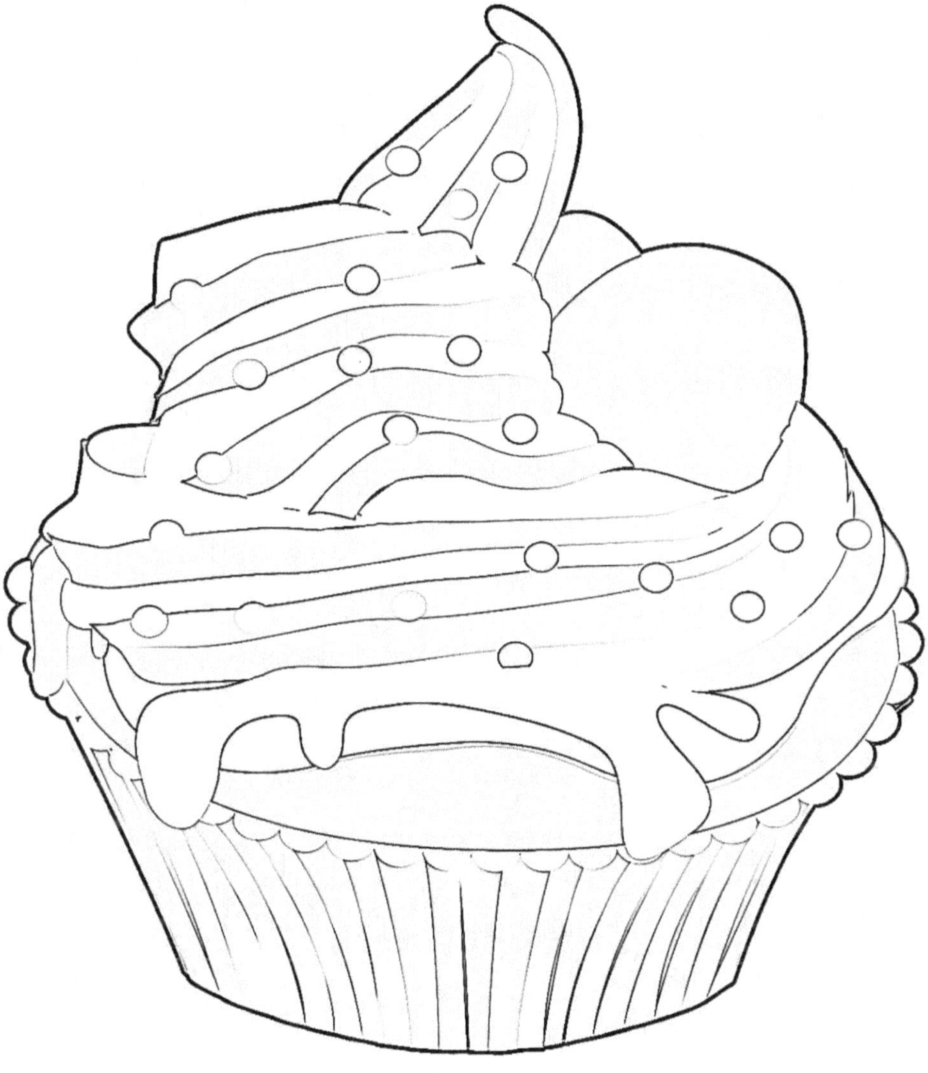

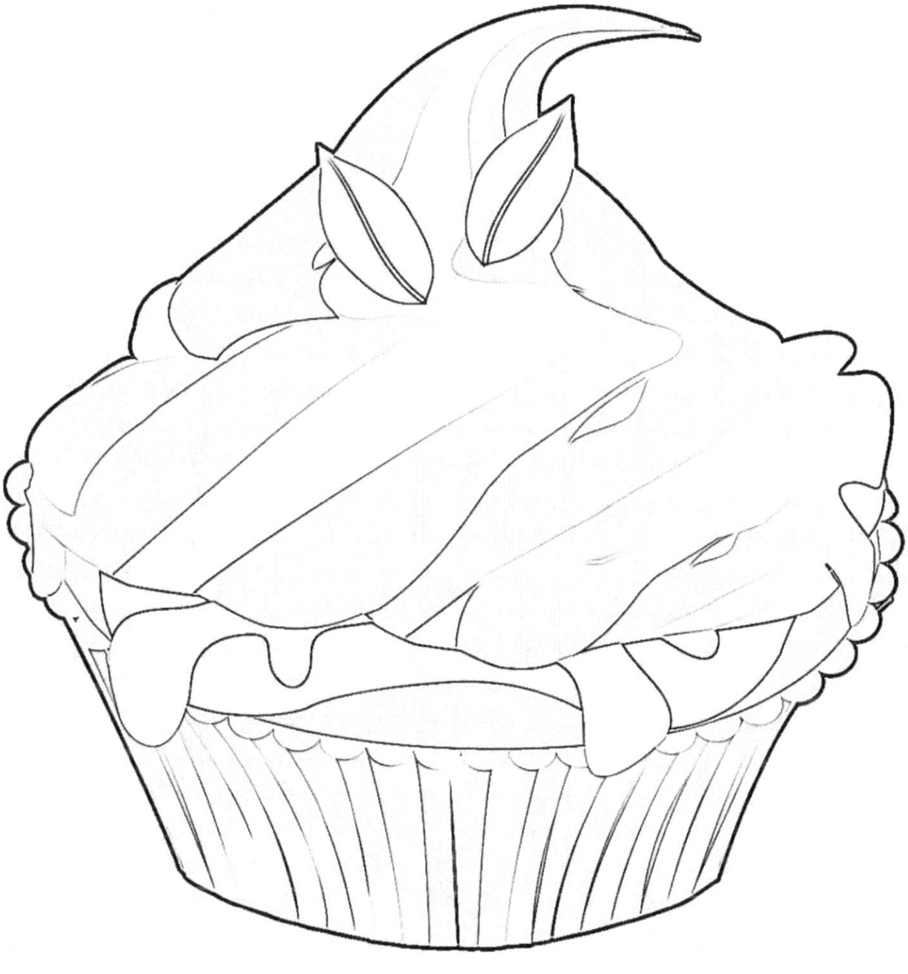

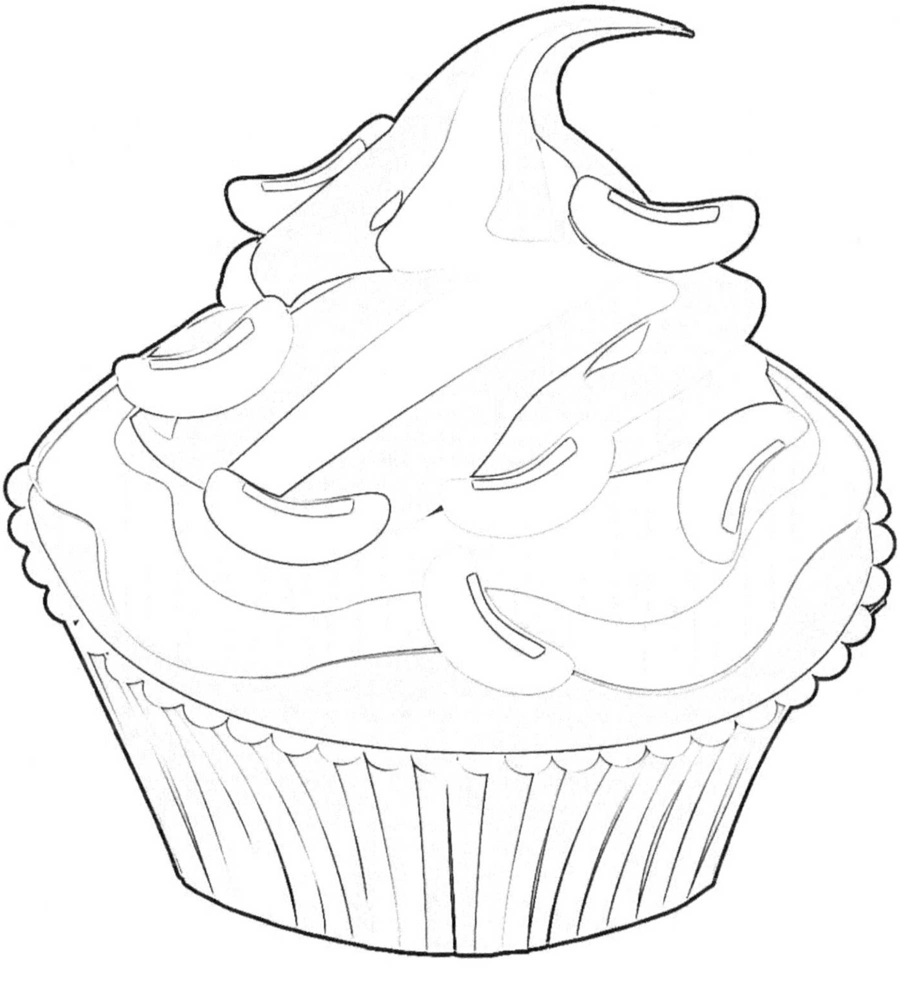

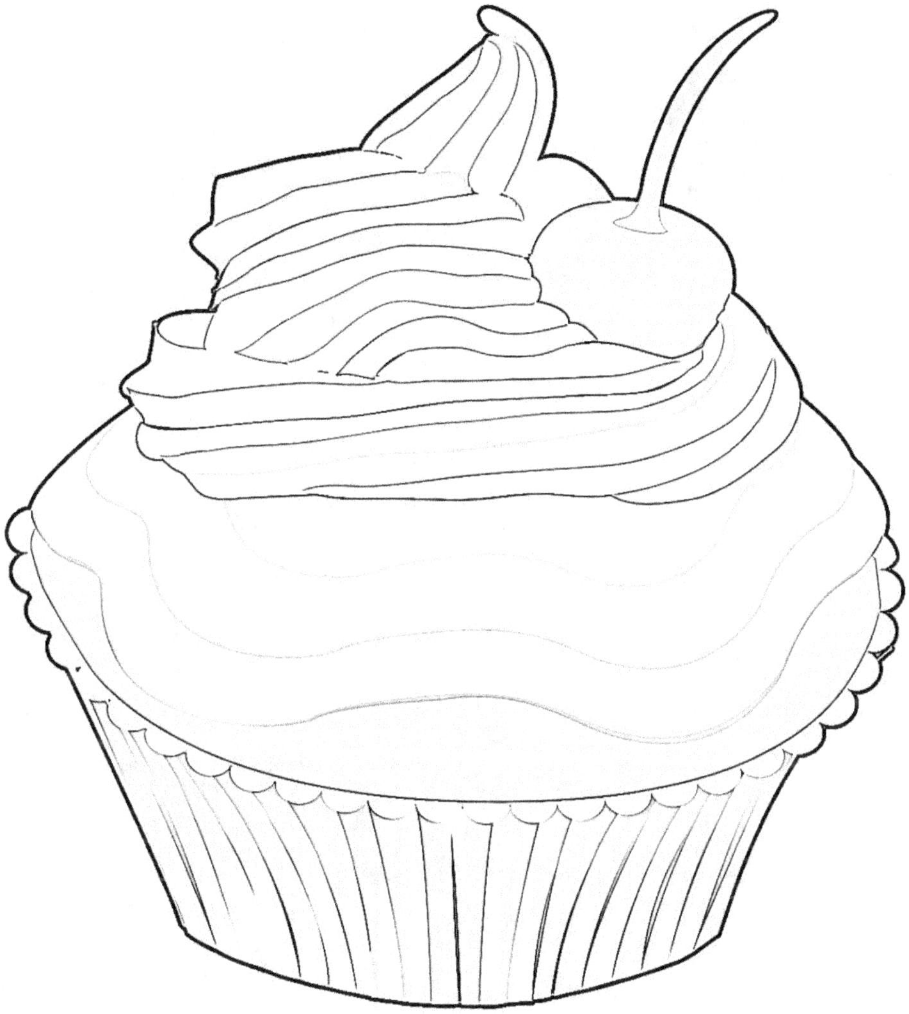

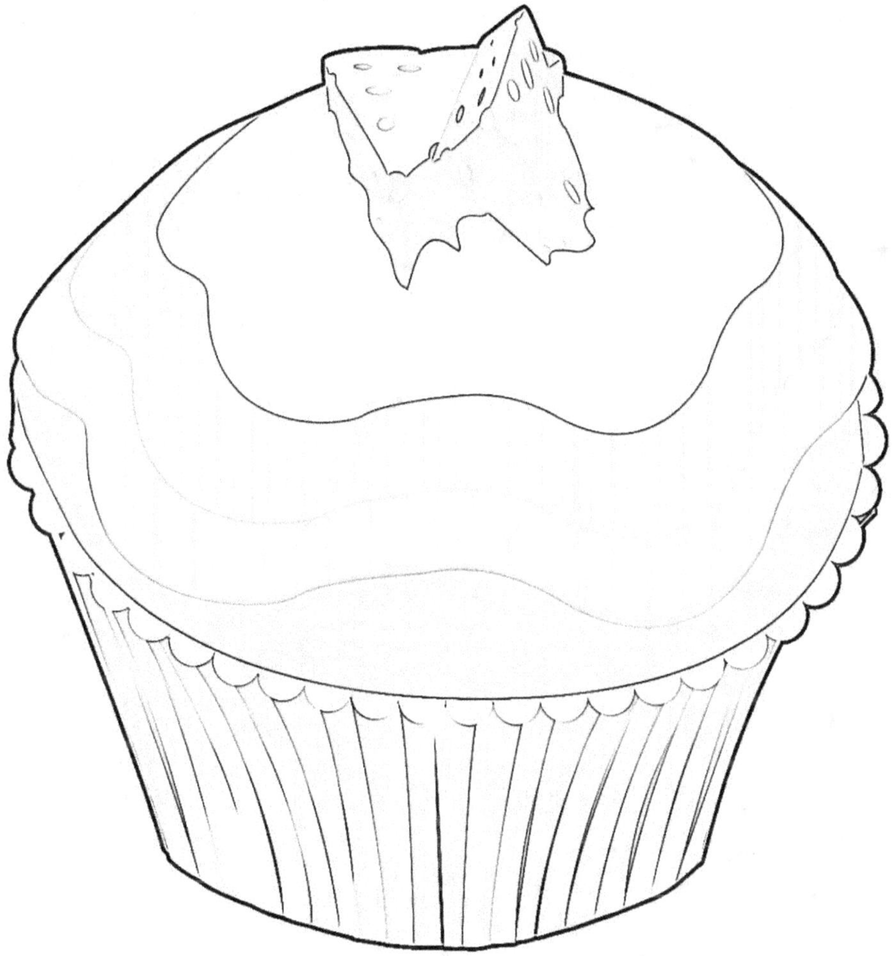

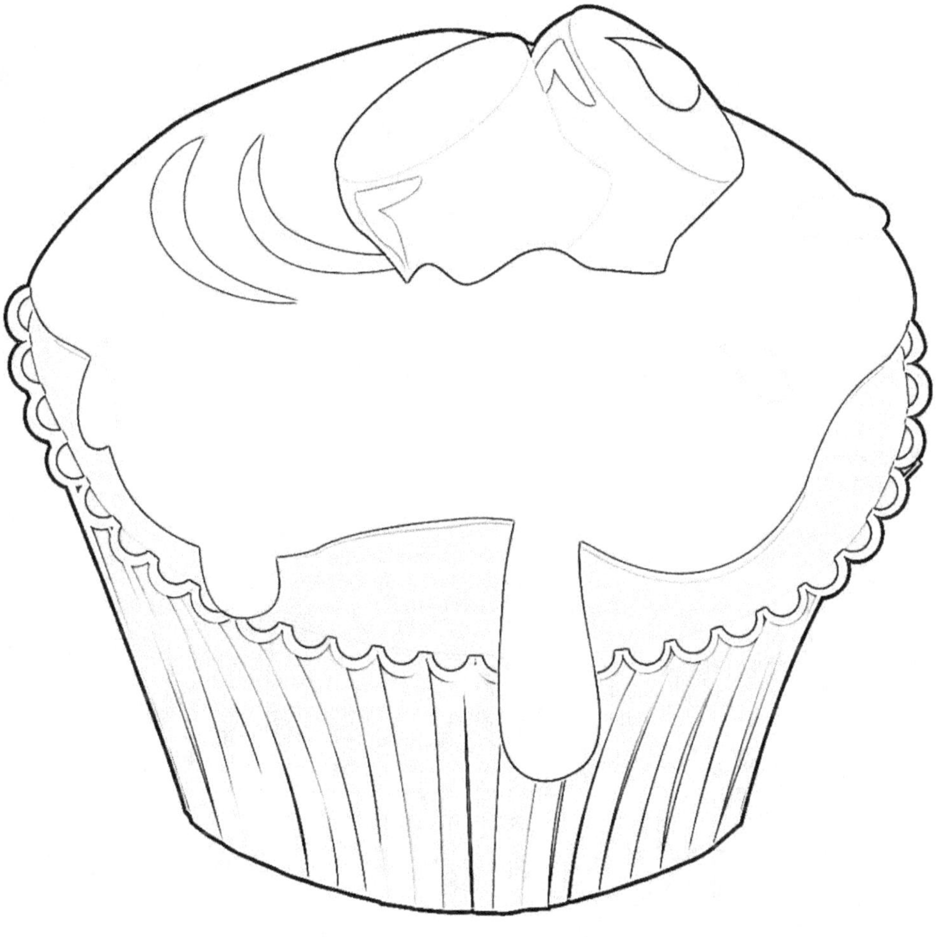

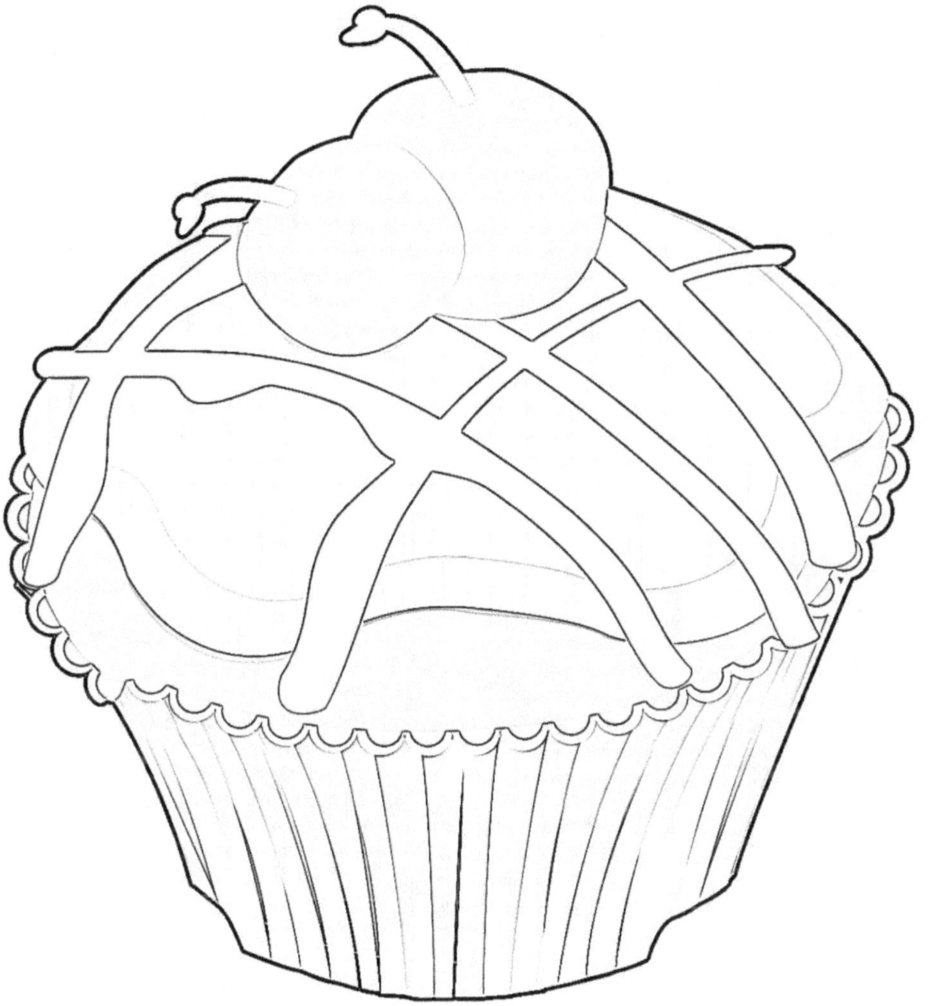

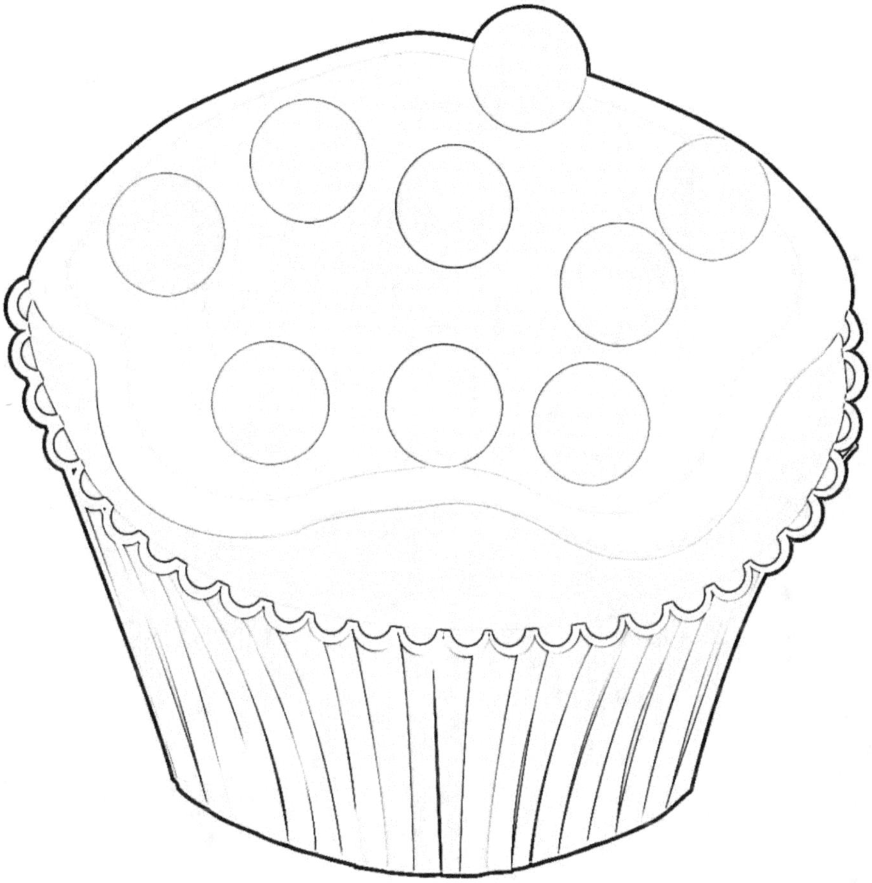

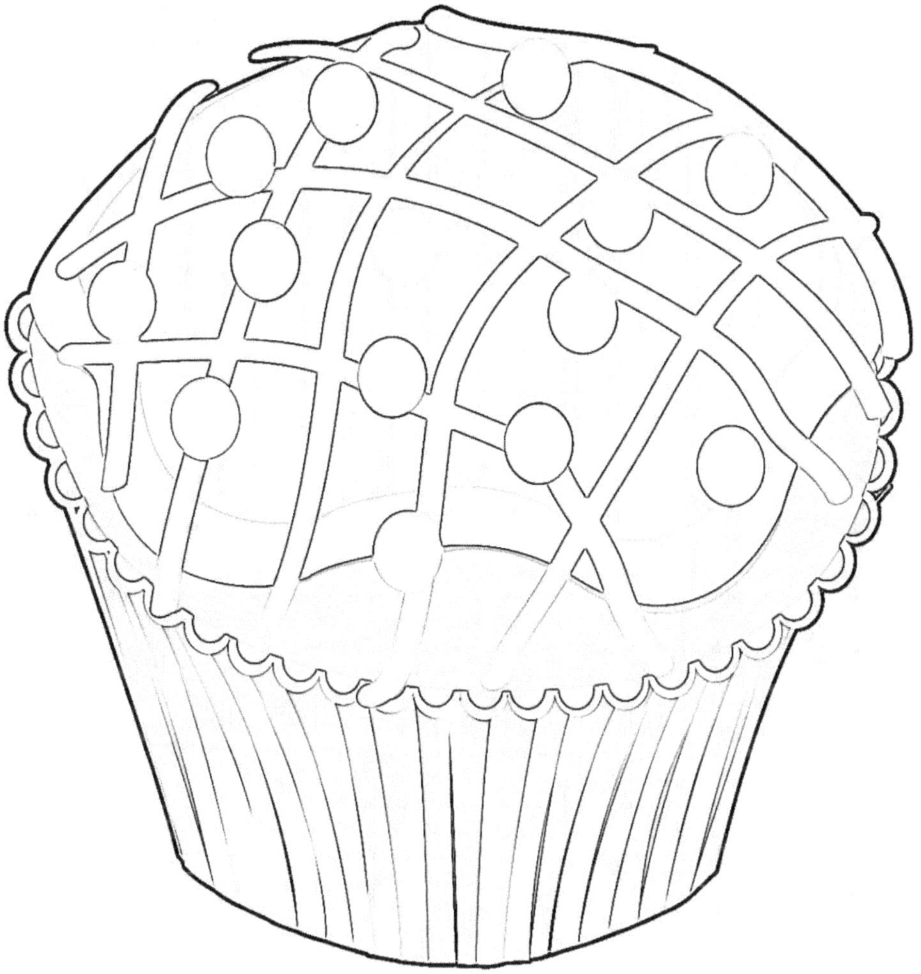

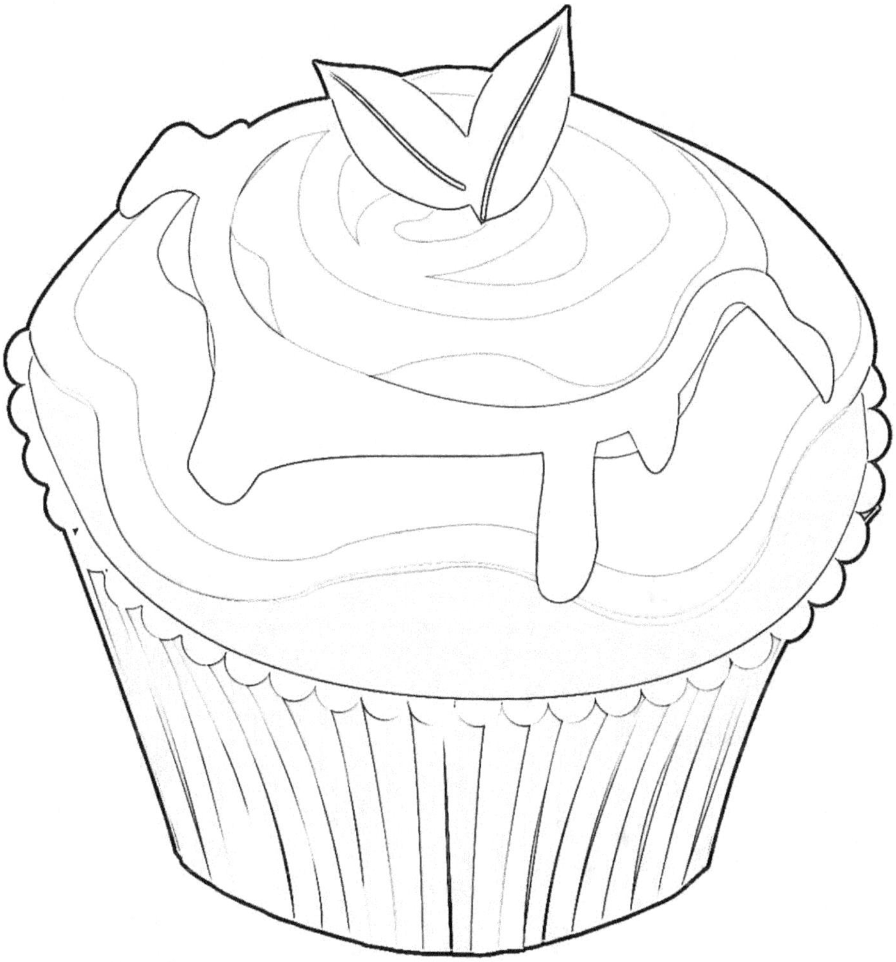

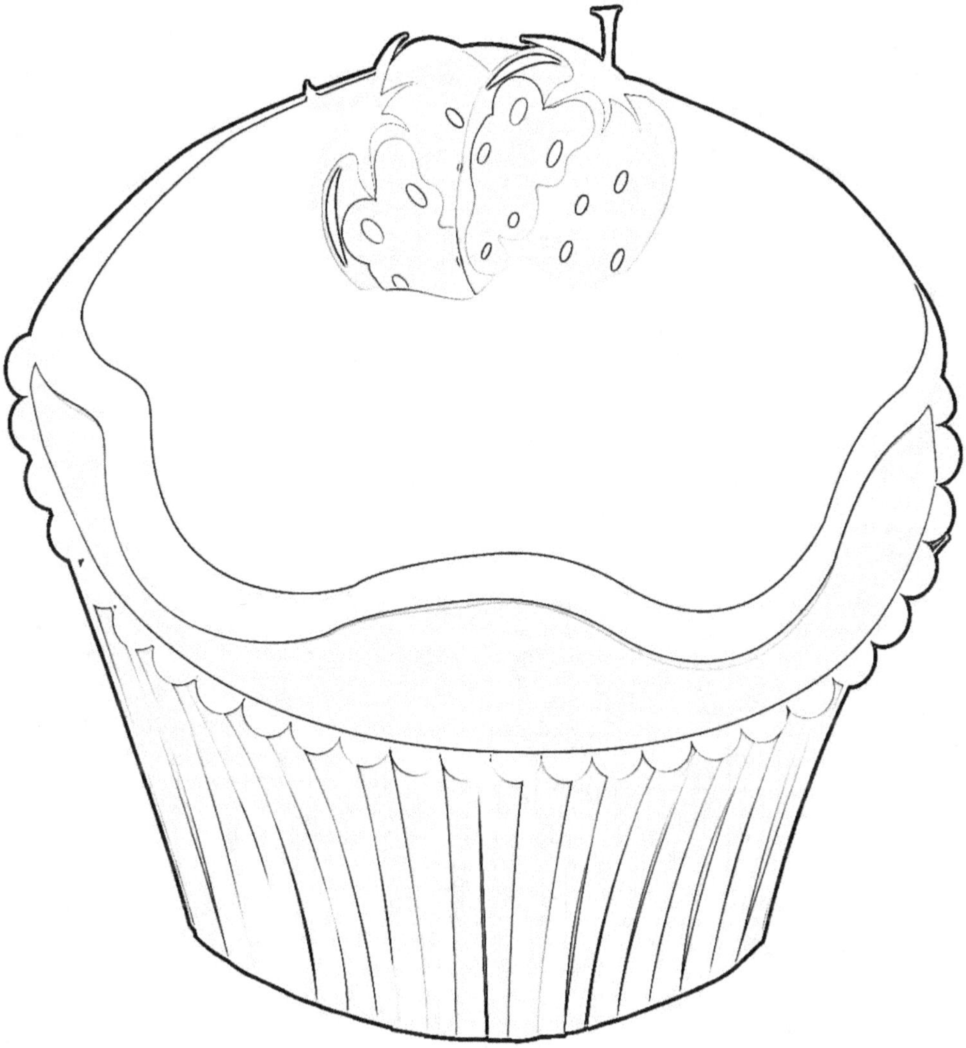

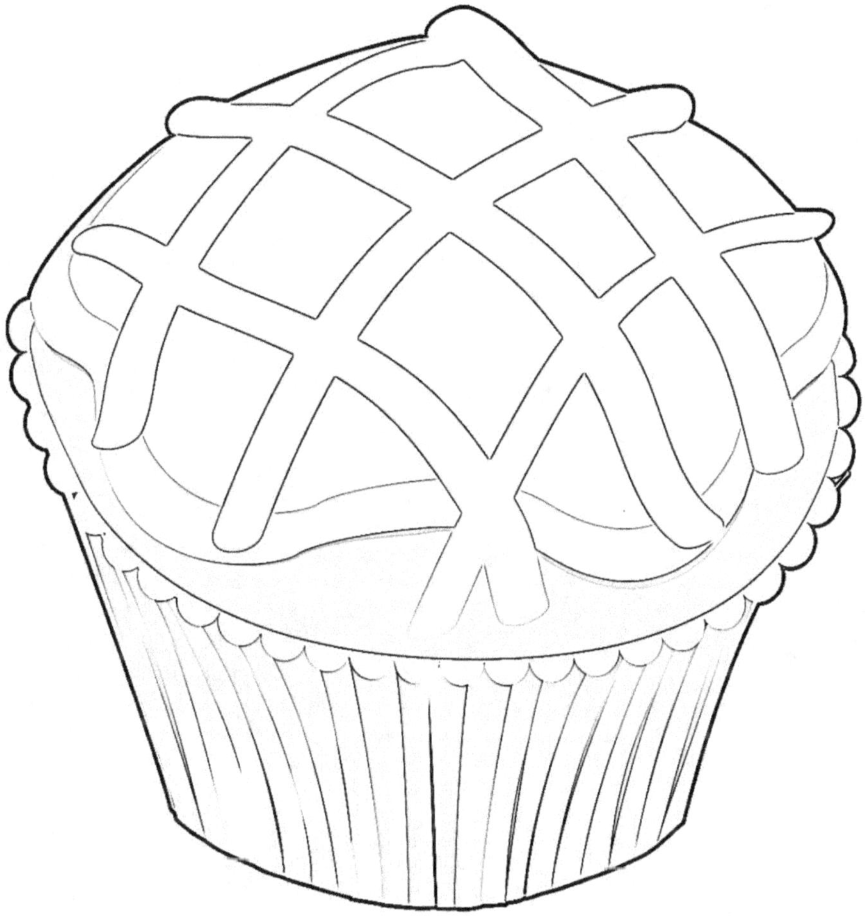

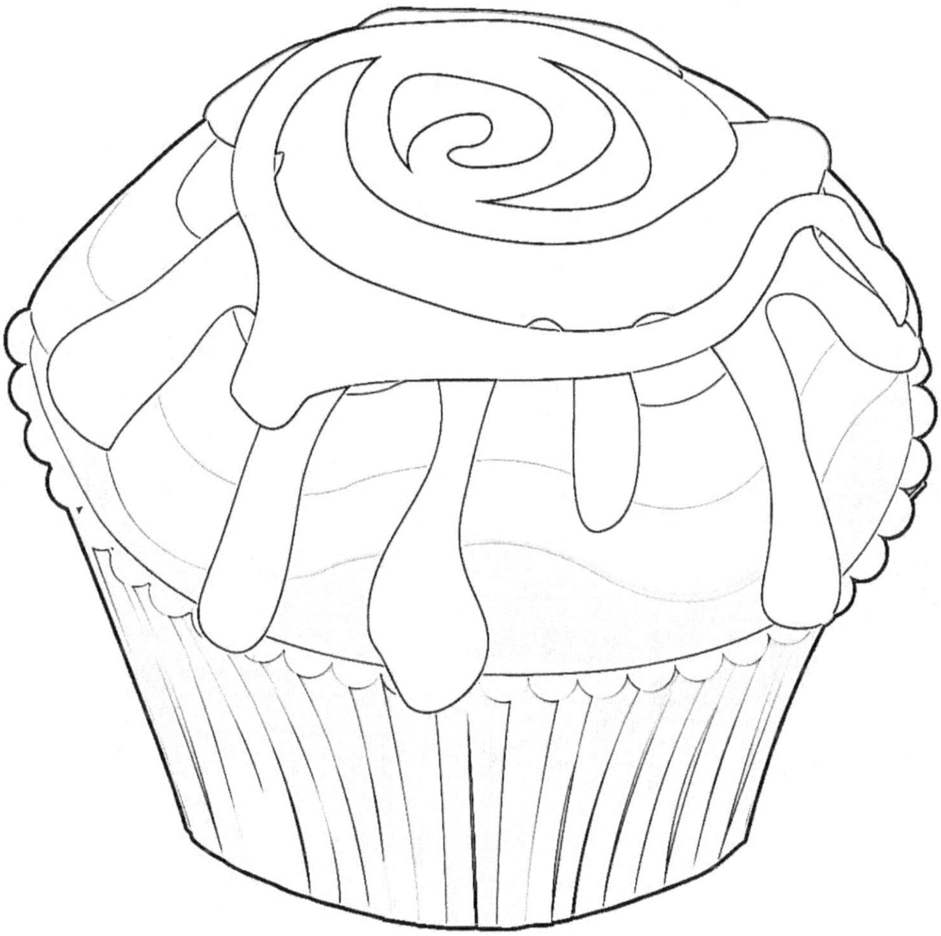

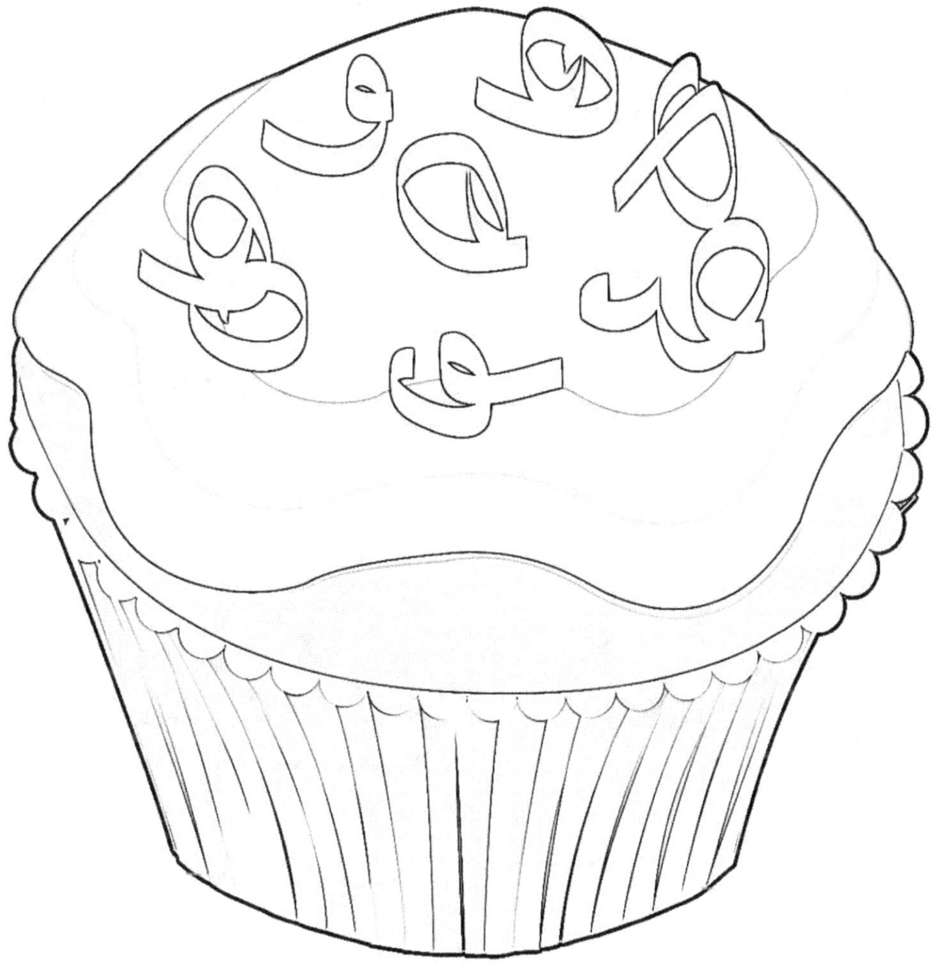

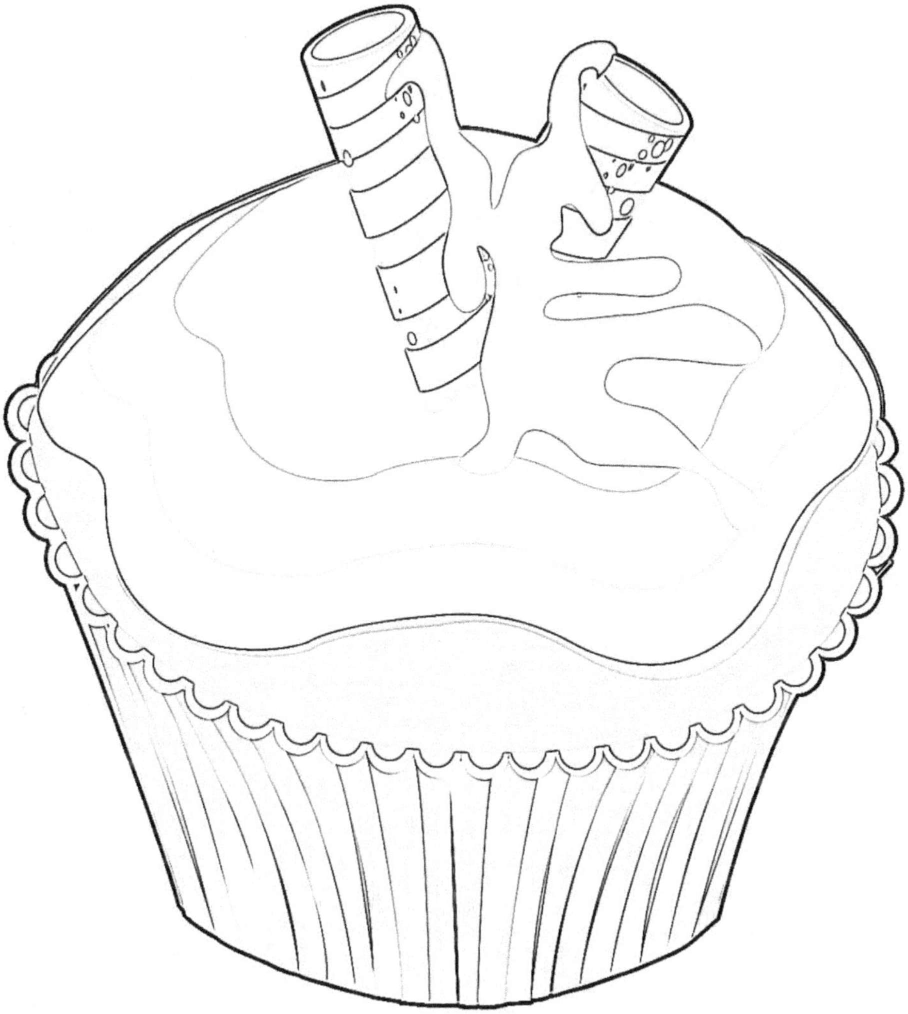

www.ingramcontent.com/pod-product-compliance
Lightning Source LLC
Chambersburg PA
CBHW081401170526
45166CB00010B/3164
* 9 7 8 1 5 1 9 5 0 9 3 5 2 *